# Plant a Garden in Your Sneaker!

Diane L. Burns

Jill A. Burns

**LEARNING
TRIANGLE
PRESS**

**An imprint of McGraw-Hill**

New York  San Francisco  Washington, D.C.  Auckland  Bogotá  Caracas
Lisbon  London  Madrid  Mexico City  Milan  Montreal  New Delhi
San Juan  Singapore  Sydney  Tokyo  Toronto

# McGraw-Hill

*A Division of The **McGraw·Hill** Companies*

Copyright© 1998 by the McGraw-Hill Companies, Inc.

Published by Learning Triangle Press, an imprint of McGraw-Hill.

1 2 3 4 5 6 7 8 9  KGP/KGP  90321098

ISBN 0-07-009228-1

McGraw-Hill books are available at special quantity discounts to use as premiums and sales promotions. For more information, please write to the Director of Special Sales, McGraw-Hill, 11 West 19th Street, New York, NY 10011. Or contact your local bookstore.

Aquisitions editor: Judith Terrill-Breuer
Production supervisor: Clare B. Stanley
Artist: Claude Martinot

# Table of Contents

## Indoor Projects

## Outdoor Projects

## Indoor or Outdoor Projects

# Acknowledgments

**Warm thanks to:**
Dawn Bassuener, who volunteered her knowledge
with humor and without reserve and painstakingly edited
all science and botany information.

**Those who answered numerous questions:**
Friends at Forth Floral: Don Kemmeter, Henning Hempel,
Marv Schumacher, Karen Sackett, Peggy Glover, and Bonnie Kofler;
also, Brent Hanson at Hanson's Rhinelander Floral;
John Kuczmarski (UW Master Gardener program instructor),
and Pat and Cheri Shields.

# Dedication

**To my grandparents,**
**Jack and Helen Christnovich and Dean and Mary Heyer,**
**who saw a gardener in a little girl.**
**Thank you for every memory.**
**—J.B.**

**To young gardeners everywhere. Dig and grow!**
**—D.B.**

# Introduction

Reading this book is like a treasure hunt: If you use the projects like a map, they will lead you down the gardening path toward a "green" thumb. Along the way, each activity uncovers fun things to do. Look for Plant Mysteries and Pro Challenges as you go!

To dig in, keep these things handy:
• newspapers to cover any indoor workspace
• tools, such as a spade, rake, trowel, and watering can
• sterilized soil for indoor plants (for outdoor projects, use garden soil, which is unsterilized)**
• a source of water
• seeds (each is a baby plant waiting to grow) and/or plants

Many of these items can be purchased from large discount stores and garden centers.

To track your gardening activities, keep a journal. In it, write down the things you did, how they turned out, what you learned, and anything you might want to do differently next time. Like other adventures, you may discover that finishing this book is really only the beginning of the fun.

**Use only sterilized soil for indoor house-plants. Unsterilized soil may contain hidden pests, such as weed seeds, fungus, or unwanted bugs. Sterilized soil has been heated to remove these, and other, unwanted things.

leaf

← stem

roots

# Sprout off!

Each seed, from the tiniest (a dustlike orchid seed) to the largest, (a kind of coconut which can weigh 40 pounds when fully grown), is a miracle waiting to grow. You can make it happen with mung bean or peppergrass seeds in a few days.

## WHAT YOU NEED:
- A double-layered, moist paper towel
- A teaspoon of untreated (chemical-free and pesticide-free) mung bean seeds. You'll find them in health-food stores.

## DIRECTIONS:

Spread the seeds on half of the moist paper towel. Fold it over and put in a warm place. Keep the towel moist. Mung seeds will germinate, or sprout, in about 5 days. When the sprouted seeds are a couple of inches long, they can be eaten. Crunchy bean sprouts taste great in sandwiches or salads.

Seed Puzzler: The size of a seed is no indication of the size of the plant it will become:

✓ Many trees begin as tiny seeds that grow into huge plants living hundreds of years;

✓ Most vegetables, whose seeds can be much larger, grow into plants a few feet in length that live only several months.

✓ To Germinate, seeds need water, oxygen, warmth, and sometimes light.

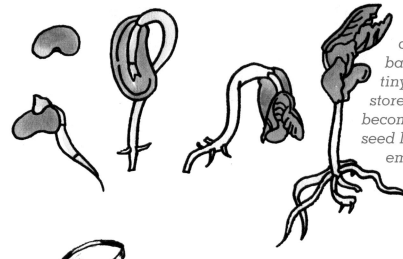

*As water softens the outer shell, called the seed coat, the embryo, or baby plant, emerges, complete with its tiny root and stem. The cotyledon is stored food, a kind of lunch bucket, which becomes the plant's first leaves. These seed leaves, held up by the stem, feed the embryo until the root begins to pull nutrients, or nourishment, from the soil and true leaves form to make food from sunlight.*

## PLANT MYSTERY

**Q.** Most seeds are hard and dry on the outside. **Why aren't they dead?**
(Answer on page 58.)

## PRO CHALLENGE

Many kinds of untreated seeds can be sprouted in larger amounts in a jar.

## WHAT YOU NEED:

- 2 tablespoons of mixed, whole, untreated seeds**
- An 8-ounce jar, filled halfway with water
- A plastic mesh top, cut from an onion bag
- A rubber band

  **choose whole alfalfa, great northern, lentil, or garbanzo bean seeds.

## DIRECTIONS:

Pour the seeds into the jar and stir. Lay the mesh across the top and secure it with the rubber band. Set the jar in a warm place. Twice a day, pour off the old water, rinse the seeds, and fill the jar with fresh water. Keep the seeds covered while they swell and split open. When the embryos are about 2 inches (5 centimeters) long, drain off the water. Put the sprouts into a container and refrigerate until you use them.

# Cutting Loose

Not all new plants are easily grown from seed. There are ways to make new plants from fully grown ones. One way is to start roots from a cut stem. This process is called layering.

## WHAT YOU NEED:

- Bobby pins
- Ivy vines still connected to a mature, disease-free plant (Most climbers and trailers with long flexible stems can be layered.)
- Rooting hormone (This helps roots form and protects the layered stem. It is available at any garden center or discount store.)
- A pot (or use your favorite old mug or cup) filled with sterilized soil

## DIRECTIONS:

1. Lightly push down the soil in the mug so that there is about 1/2-inch (1 centimeter) space at the top.
2. Select 3 ivy vines about 8 to 10 inches (20 to 25 centimeters) long.
3. Carefully make a small nick in each vine where you want it to root (about 3 inches or 8 centimeters back from the tip). Be careful not to cut through the vine. Lay the vine across the surface of the mug, and carefully pin it down with a bobby pin or two. Do not cut the vine from the parent plant.

4. Make sure that both the parent and the layered plants are in bright indirect sunlight, which means that the sun shines near the plant but not on it. Water the layered ivy so the soil is moist, not soaked.

5. When your layered ivies begin to root, new growth will appear. The plant will now grow on its own. Cut the connecting stem between it and the parent plant.

*Be patient! The layering process takes a couple of months to produce roots. Don't peek to see if roots are forming because removing the vines from their place may destroy them.*

## PLANT MYSTERY

**Q.** Cotyledons provide food for a seed's embryo. Leaf cuttings do not have cotyledons, and their new roots will take time to develop. **What provides the food for your layered cutting?** (Answer on page 58.)

## PRO CHALLENGE

Grow an African violet from a cutting, which is a healthy, disease-free mature leaf with an attached stem, taken from its parent plant.

# Look'in Glass

Grow an enclosed rain forest and prove that plants breathe!

## WHAT YOU NEED:

- A clean small aquarium with cover
- 3 to 5 small low-light houseplants such as ferns, mosses, neanthe bella palm, dracaena, prayer plant, aluminum plant, or magic carpet plant
- Pebbles
- Wood charcoal
- Sand
- A spoon
- Moist sterilized soil
- A cork or spool attached to a stick

## DIRECTIONS:

1. Arrange a 1-inch (2½- centimeter) layer of pebbles on the bottom of the aquarium or container. This makes needed air space and allows excess water to drain away from the plant roots.

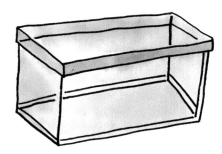

2. Spread a 1-inch (2½-centimeter) layer of sand on top of the pebbles.

3. Spread a ½-inch (1-centimeter) layer of wood charcoal on top of the sand and gravel.

4. Top the charcoal with 1 inch (2½-centimeters) of soil. Use the spoon to gently place the soil into the corners.

5. Set plants gently onto the soil in a pattern that allows you to see them from any angle. Fill in any empty spots with more soil. The soil surface should be about one-fourth the height of the container.
6. Firm the soil gently around the plants. Use a cork or spool attached to a stick as a tamper for hard-to-reach areas.
7. Place the cap or cover on your terrarium and set in indirect sunlight.

✓ Landscape: Add a small mirror for a lake, miniature animal figurines, bridges, or other small items.

*If the terrarium fogs up, uncover it until the water vapor disappears, then cover it again. Never add water to your terrarium unless the soil dries out. This is because a living plant's leaves act as "lungs," and respirate, or give off, water vapor. This respirating process is called transpiration. Leaves also give off oxygen—so thank a plant today for helping you breathe.*

## PLANT MYSTERY

**Q.** The hydrologic, or rain, cycle occurs over and over inside a terrarium. **How does it help your plants grow?** (Answer on page 58.)

*continued on next page*

Make a terrarium by putting rooted cuttings through the narrow opening of a soda bottle.

## WHAT YOU NEED:

- A 2-liter plastic soda bottle with a cap
- Rooted plant cuttings (do not use cacti or succulents)
- Long tweezers or chopsticks
- An old baby spoon or small plastic spoon taped to a narrow stick
- Unsterilized soil, pebbles, and sand
- Rolled-up newspaper for a funnel
- Patience!!!

## DIRECTIONS:

1. Place the bottle upright and take off the cap. Using your paper funnel, sift 1 inch (2½-centimeters) each of pebbles and sand into the bottom of the bottle. Then sift 2 inches (5 centimeters) of soil on top of the sand. Push down the soil lightly with the spoon.

2. With the tweezers, carefully push 2 to 4 cuttings onto the soil. Make sure the roots are completely covered.

3. Water the plants until the soil is moist, then place the cap back on.

4. If your plants get too large for the container, carefully cut through the middle of the bottle to create two halves. Remove the overgrown plants, replace them with smaller ones, and secure the halves together again with masking tape.

# It's A Dry Life

Everyone knows that cacti don't need a lot of care because they're desert plants. What about succulents? They, too, are easy to care for and don't require much water. Why else would they be called "plant camels"?

## WHAT YOU NEED:

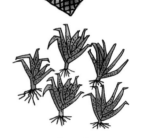

- A clean, shallow 4- to 6-inch clay flowerpot with a drainage hole and saucer
- A piece of screen to cover the drainage hole
- Perlite or small pebbles
- Light textured sterilized soil
- 4 to 6 young aloe plants, called offsets**

** Baby look-alikes: Offsets are young versions of some types of parent plants.

## DIRECTIONS:

1. Place the screen on the bottom of the clay pot.
2. Pour 1 inch (2½-centimeters) of perlite or pebbles in the bottom of the clay pot. Be careful not to move the screen.
3. Fill the pot with soil and push down, or tamp,

slightly. Plant the aloe offsets 1 inch (2½-centimeters) apart and deep enough to cover the roots well. Fill in any empty spots with soil.
4. Place the clay pot on the saucer in bright indirect sunlight. Wait a week before watering to give broken or damaged roots time to heal and take up water properly.
5. Water when the soil is dry to the touch. Drain out any water in the saucer because succulents rot easily.

*Aloe is great for healing cuts, scrapes, or burns. Cut off a small piece and squeeze the juices directly onto the wound.*

6. Aloe plants will grow and produce offsets. If your plants get too crowded, divide them and repot some for your friends and neighbors. Remember to fill in any holes with more soil.

## PLANT MYSTERY

**Q. How do cacti and succulents protect themselves from animals, weather, and other dangers?**
(Answer on page 58.)

# PRO CHALLENGE

Nature designed succulents so that they could grow from seed and also from plant parts such as thick, fleshy leaves, stems, or branches where water is stored. This allows the plant to survive during dry weather, or drought. To grow a plant camel of your own, all you need is one jade leaf and a little patience.

## DIRECTIONS:

1. Carefully pull off several healthy leaves from the bottom of a large jade plant. Allow the leaves to dry for 2 to 3 days. Then, follow directions 1 to 3 above.
2. Lay the leaves on the soil surface and press lightly onto the soil. Water until the soil is moist and whenever it's dry on top.
3. When the leaves form new plants, remove the starter leaves and transplant the young jades into their own pots.

# Winter Light Bulbs

Bulbs will bloom between December and January if you start this project from the middle of September to the first of October.

## WHAT YOU NEED:

- 5 or 6 paperwhite narcissus or hyacinth bulbs
- A wide shallow container such as a discarded lunchbox
- Pebbles
- Water

## DIRECTIONS:

1. Fill the lunchbox with pebbles up to 2 inches (5 centimeters) from the top. Gently scoop 5 or 6 hollows in the pebbles. Bury the bulbs, root side down, about 1/2 inch (1 centimeter) apart, one to a hollow, so that the necks are showing. Pour enough water to cover the pebbles but not enough to overflow the sides of the container or drown the bulbs.

2. Place the container in a cool, dark room until the bulbs start to sprout. Make sure you check the water level every day so the bulbs' roots don't dry out. When the sprouts are about 3 inches (7 to 8 centimeters) high, move the lunchbox to bright indirect light. (Keeping the container out of direct sunlight will allow your plants and flowers to last longer.)

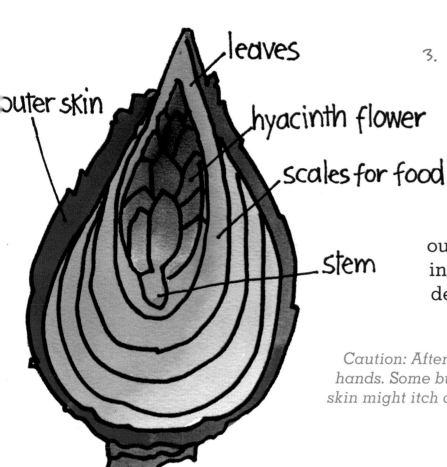

leaves

outer skin

hyacinth flower

scales for food

stem

3. After the blooms fade and the leaves turn brown, or wilt, throw out the paperwhite narcissus bulbs. They can be grown only once. Hyacinths, however, can be planted in an outdoor garden about 4 to 6 inches (10 to 15 centimeters) deep.

*Caution: After handling any bulb, wash your hands. Some bulbs are toxic if tasted, and your skin might itch after handling hyacinth bulbs.*

✓ Look, Mom! No Soil!: Bulbs such as hyacinths, daffodils, and tulips are known as true bulbs. They produce offsets attached to the parent bulb, which can be separated and planted in their own space. If you slice a bulb open, you will see the roots, stems, leaves, and flowers inside. Scales hidden beneath the papery outside layer of the bulb provide protection and food.

## PLANT MYSTERY

**Q.** A bulb's leaves stay green for weeks long after it has flowered. Removing the leaves before they turn brown and wither harms the bulb. **How can the health of this year's leaves affect next year's flowers?** (Answer on page 58.)

*continued on next page*

✓ "Lighten Up": If your paperwhites start to bend over, they aren't getting enough light. If this happens, move the container to bright indirect light. Wrap a string around the plant and tie it to a stick. Hyacinths, too, get top-heavy and may need to be propped up.

✓ Trick-or-Treat: Daffodil and tulips can be "tricked" into blooming. This is called forcing. Cool temperatures provide healthy root growth at a faster rate.

✓ "May the Force be with You!": Once the flowers fade, move the pot to a cool, sunny spot. Depending on where you live, most bulbs that are forced indoors cannot be forced again but can be planted outdoors, where they might bloom the next year.

## PRO CHALLENGE

It would take about 40 years to plant all the kinds of tulip or daffodil bulbs in the world if you planted a different one every day! Compared to that, this project will take no time at all!

## WHAT YOU NEED:

- 3 or 4 daffodil or tulip bulbs (bigger ones produce the nicest plants)
- A clean 6-inch pot with drainage holes
- A deflated sports ball such as a basketball, soccer ball, or volleyball with the top cut off
- Moistened sterilized soil
- Water

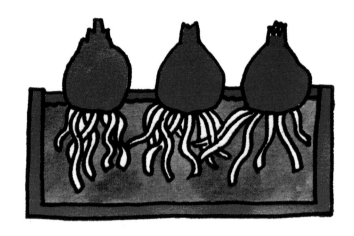

## DIRECTIONS:

1. Fill the pot to the rim with soil. Bury the bulbs, root side down, with their necks slightly showing. Place the potted bulbs in the refrigerator for 8 to 10 weeks. Monitor the moisture of the soil. If it dries out while in the refrigerator, the plant might not produce flowers.

2. After the cooling period, take the pot out of the refrigerator and place it in the sports ball. By now, the plants have pushed their way through the soil surface. Slowly reintroduce the bulbs to warmth and light. For 10 days, place the pot in a 60 to 65 degree room with indirect sunlight. After that, place it where you can enjoy the flowers.

# Lettuce Eat!

"Green" and bear it! Lettuce leaves, which are 95 percent water, aren't just for rabbits. So, "What's up, Doc?" Three unusual greens in your indoor salad!

## WHAT YOU NEED:

- A narrow shoebox lined with heavy plastic and filled with moist, sterilized soil
- 1 packet of peppergrass seeds
- 6 white or yellow onion bulbs, called sets
- 1 packet of black-seeded Simpson leaf lettuce seeds

- Three clean popsicle sticks labeled (1) peppergrass (2) onion and (3) lettuce
- Pebbles

## DIRECTIONS:

1. Press your finger lightly into the soil to divide it into three areas. Sow peppergrass seeds in one of the areas by pressing them lightly into the soil. Mark this area with the first popsicle stick.
2. In a second area, evenly space the onion bulbs, root side down, about half a finger's depth into the soil. Mark this area with the second popsicle stick.
3. In the last area, press the lettuce seeds just beneath the surface and lightly cover with soil. Mark this area with the third popsicle stick.

4. Set the planter in a sunny window. When the surface of the soil is dry to the touch, sprinkle with water without disturbing the seeds. Soaking the soil will rot the seeds. Lettuce sprouts may be thinned,
or spaced, by removing crowded sprouts so that the ones left behind have enough room
to grow.

## PLANT MYSTERY

**Q.** Garden seeds, stored in a cool, dry place, will keep for up to a year before they are used. **Why don't they germinate on the shelf?** (Answer on page 58.)

Other edible herbs and greens can be found at:
Nichols Garden Nursery
1190 North Pacific Highway
Albany, OR 97321
The Cook's Garden
P.O. Box 535
Londonderry, VT 05148

*Mustardy-tasting peppergrass, also called curly grass or garden cress, germinates in 1 day and is ready to harvest in 2 weeks. It's so eager to get going, that it will even sprout between damp paper towels and doesn't mind being crowded.

* Red and green leaf lettuces can be harvested in 5 weeks. Pinch off whole leaves and wash them before eating. Be careful not to pull up the roots; if they are not damaged, the lettuce will continue to grow. Like the green kinds, red leaf lettuces have chlorophyll, but their red pigment hides the green.

* To harvest an onion after 3 to 4 weeks, pull it up by the root. Wash and peel the bulb, cut off the roots, and chop the greens and bulb into your salad.

*continued on next page*

# PRO  CHALLENGE

Aren't they cute? We're not talking baby animals here, but about baby veggies! Eat them whole or on your salad greens.

## WHAT YOU NEED:
- 1 pinch thumbelina carrot seeds
- 1 pinch Easter egg radish seeds
- 3 bush pickle seeds
- A medium to large wooden crate lined with heavy plastic that has been punctured on the bottom for drainage and filled with moist sterilized soil
- 3 clean popsicle sticks labeled
    (1) carrots,
    (2) radishes, and
    (3) bush pickles

## DIRECTIONS:

1. Set the soil-filled crate in a sunny spot outdoors. With your finger, divide the soil into three places. Place the labeled popsicle sticks in the soil, one to an area. Sow the carrot and radish seeds in the appropriate areas. Space the bush pickle seeds 2 inches apart from each other. Cover all the seeds lightly with soil.

2. As the carrots and radishes grow, they may need to be thinned. Bush pickles like to stretch. It's okay if they grow over the side of the crate. Mark your calendar for eating: Radishes will be ready to pull up in about a month; bush pickles can be picked from the vine in about a month and a half; carrots can be pulled up in about two and a half months. Nobody wants a mouthful of dirt, so remember to wash the veggies before munching!

# Plant Pets!

Grow your own insectivorous plant and watch a meat-eating mystery. Don't shoo those pesky flies out of your house. Your plant will act as a natural flyswatter (and it won't leave fly guts on your wall!).

## WHAT YOU NEED:

- Venus flytrap plant **(buy at a garden center or source below)
- A 2-liter clear plastic soda bottle with a cap
- Masking tape
- Pebbles
- Sphagnum moss
- Rain water or distilled water only, not tap water
- Scissors

***Note: Venus flytraps can be ordered from:*
*Northwoods Plant Pets*
*P.O.Box 1703*
*Eagle River WI 54521*
*1-800-737-9787*

# DIRECTIONS:

1. Using scissors, cut through the middle of the soda bottle to form two halves. Set the upper half aside.

2. Holding the lower half upright, pour 1 inch (2½ centimeters) of pebbles into the bottom. Form the sphagnum moss into a bird nest on top of the pebbles.

3. Gently wrap sphagnum moss around the roots of the flytrap and set the root ball into the bird nest. Moisten the moss carefully. Too much water will rot the bulb.

4. Snugly fit the top over the bottom by gently squeezing the sides of the bottle and tape the two pieces together. Because your pet needs a lot of humidity, keep the cap on at all times, except when feeding or watering.

5. Place your pet plant in an east or west exposure that receives 6 to 10 hours of indirect sunlight. Flytraps grow best in a steady 60 to 80 degree temperature.

*Feed your plant live flies, spiders, ants, or gnats once a week. Take off the cap and put the insect inside the bottle. Fertilizing or using tap water (which has added chemicals) may harm the plant.*

← sphagnum moss

← pebbles

*Venus flytraps may go dormant. If this happens, don't water the plant. Cut off any dead leaves or traps. Wipe clean both the bulb (being careful not to scratch it) and the container. For 8 to 10 weeks, store the bulb in the refrigerator undisturbed. Remove it and replant in new sphagnum moss.*

*continued on next page*

# VENUS FLYTRAP TIPS:

1. Snip off old black traps, and new traps will grow. Red inside walls means that the plant is getting plenty of bright indirect light.

2. Traps that form at the end of a leaf are small on new plants and larger on older ones. Tickling the traps weakens the plant.

3. Venus flytraps are sometimes sold as bulbs. Small and large bulbs grow at about the same rate.

4. Do not feed hamburger or other meats to your pet. Extra protein and fat will kill it.

5. The flytrap secretes sweet aromas that lead the unsuspecting insect close. The trap closes tighter and tighter until its meal is sealed in an airtight pocket. Enzymes pour out, drowning and digesting the insect. The process takes 4 to 20 days. When the trap reopens, it might have a shell of the insect inside because, just like humans, the plant doesn't eat bones.

## PLANT MYSTERY

**Q.** Venus flytrap roots are surrounded by water and sphagnum moss instead of soil. **Since it shouldn't be fertilized, where does the plant get its nutrients?** (Answer on page 59.)

# PRO CHALLENGE

When your Venus flytrap flowers, you will have an opportunity to grow new plants. Or order from the address below.**

1. After the flowers wilt, seed pods will form and turn brownish-black. When the seeds inside are ripe and dry, cut off the flower stalks.

2. Cut open the pods and shake the seeds onto a white piece of paper so that you can see them (they are very small). Store them in a plastic sandwich bag and place it in the refrigerator until you are ready to sow the seeds.

3. In a blender, chop up enough sphagnum moss to fill the container you choose, leaving 1 inch (2½ centimeters) at the top.

4. Sprinkle the seeds on top of the moss, then cover with another layer of chopped moss.

5. Mist the moss thoroughly and cover with a plastic bag. Place the covered container on a sunny windowsill.

6. Be patient. It may take several months for the seeds to germinate. Keeping the moss moist at all times helps the seeds to sprout more quickly. When tiny traps appear, take off the plastic bag to feed the plants fruitflies and other tiny bugs. After feeding, replace the plastic bag.

*\*\*Note: Venus flytrap seeds can be ordered from:*
*George W. Parks Seed Co., Inc.*
*1 Parkton Avenue*
*Greenwood, S.C. 29647-0001*
*1-800-845-3369*

# Make Your Bed!

Pet earthworms are the best-kept secret for feeding your plants, indoors and out!

## WHAT YOU NEED:

- A 10-gallon plastic storage container with cover
- A shallow-sided drainage pan, large enough to hold the plastic container
- 10 pounds of black-and-white newspaper (a stack 4 inches [10 centimeters] high), shredded into 1-inch (2½-centimeter) strips
- A clean, 5-quart ice cream pail half filled with unsterilized soil
- 4 cups of fruit and vegetable peelings and used coffee grounds (needed each day)
- 2 gallons (7½ liters) of water
- 100 red worms** (buy at bait shops or other places that carry fishing supplies, or order from the source on the next page)

*Order by mail:*
*Worms Way  7850 N. Hwy 37*
*Bloomington,  IN  47404*
     *1-800-274-9676*

*\*\*Red worms and nightcrawlers are both*
*earthworms, but nightcrawlers do not*
     *do well indoors, nor do they eat enough to*
*make much vermicompost, or worm castings*
*(poop).  Use red worms only, because they eat their*
*own weight in food every day.  A robin isn't fussy.  It will*
*eat any kind of earthworm—up to 14 feet (4¹/4 meters) of them a day!*

## DIRECTIONS:

1. With adult help, drill 10 to 15 air holes, each about ¹/4 inch
   (¹/2 centimeter) wide, into the bottom of the plastic container.
   This is the worm bed.  Set it on the drainage container in an
   area that is between 50 and 75 degrees (a basement is the best
   place).

✓ Escape Artists!:  Because worms can wiggle out, tape screening
over the holes.

2. Mix together the
   shredded news-
   paper and soil
   in the worm
   bed.  The soil
   helps the worms
   to digest their
   food.

*continued on next page*

3. Add water slowly until the worm bedding is moist, not dripping. Do not add more water until the bedding begins to dry. Any water that drains out the bottom should be removed to prevent bad odors. It is great to use for watering plants.

4. Make a "worm sandwich" by putting moist bedding above and below, with the worms in the middle so that they don't dry out.

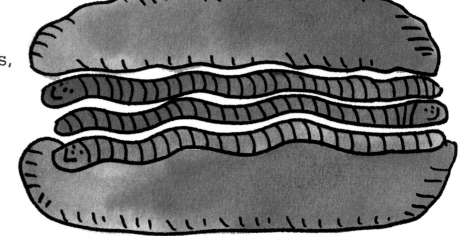

5. To feed your worms, make a hole in a corner of the bedding and bury the food scraps, alternating sides each day. To prevent the bedding from smelling bad, drop in additional moist bedding every couple of months.

✓ Population Explosion!: Young earthworms can mate in just 3 months. Put any extra wigglers into your garden or lawn.

PLANT MYSTERY 1

**Q.** To an earthworm, a dandelion's root is a combination jackhammer and elevator. **Explain how this is true.** (Answer on page 59.)

## PRO CHALLENGE

Eventually, the worm's bedding will begin to turn into an earthy-smelling vermicompost, which is used to feed plants. To remove this plant food without disturbing the worms, scoop all the bedding to one side of the container, and put new moist bedding on the empty side. Add food scraps each day and wait 4 or 5 weeks for the worms to switch sides. Now you're able to scoop out the vermicompost. Fill the empty space with new moist bedding and food scraps.

Make a fertile soil for all plants using vermicompost. Mix equal amounts of worm castings, unsterilized garden soil, perlite, and peat moss in a large container. It is best used outdoors. If used indoors, pull out any weeds that grow.

## PLANT MYSTERY 2

**Q. What part of an earthworm's body allows it to see and breathe?**
(Answer on page 59.)

# Stumped!

Nature makes her own recyclable "containers" from hollow stumps, logs, and cracks in both living and dead trees.

## WHAT YOU NEED:

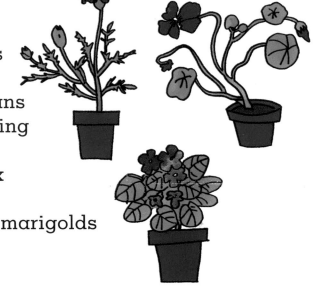

- A hollow, wooden cavity, such as an old stump or log about 8 inches (20 centimeters) deep.
- Several annual plants (which means that they live and die in one growing season):
  Shade: vinca vine, impatiens, wax begonias, coleus
  Sun: nasturtium, alyssum, salvia, marigolds
- Soil

## DIRECTIONS:

1. Fill the stump cavity with soil. With your hand, scoop one hole for each plant.
2. Center the annual in the hole and firm soil around the roots. Put taller plants in the back and vining ones at the front so that they can spill over the sides as they grow.

3. Water the soil when it is dry to the touch.

## PLANT MYSTERY

**Q. Why does a living tree die when a strip of bark is pulled off all the way around the trunk?** (Answer on page 59.)

✓ Animal Hotel! Dead trees are important to birds and other small animals. In the outdoors, about half of all wild animal homes are dead and dying trees.

## PRO CHALLENGE

You can tell a tree's age when you study a newly sawn stump that has been cut straight across. Each dark ring stands for one year in the tree's life. If the dark rings are close together, there was a series of dry, stressful years. Rings that are wide apart mean wetter, easier years. Starting at the center, count until you get to the ring before the bark. The number you get equals the tree's age.

# The Lawn and Short of It

Not every artist needs paper and pencil. You can grow a picture in your lawn. This project is for a colorful rocket. Use your imagination to plant others.

## WHAT YOU NEED:

- A ball of string
- 5 wooden or plastic tent stakes
- A sunny, level spot in your lawn, about 18 inches (1/2 meter) wide and 3 feet (1 meter) long
- Annual seeds for color:
  1 packet of white alyssum for the top nose of the rocket
  2 packets of moss roses for the body of the rocket
  1 packet of marigold seeds for the bottom flames of the rocket
- A rubber mallet or small hammer

30

# DIRECTIONS:

1. At each of the four corners of a rectangle, (about 18 inches by 3 feet, or ½ meter by 1 meter), pound one stake halfway into the ground with the mallet.
Tie string snugly all the way around. This is the base of the rocket.

2. To form the rocket's nose, pound the remaining stake at the top as shown in the figure.
Tie string around it to form a triangle.

3. Prepare a garden space by digging up the ground inside the string and raking it smooth. Sow the seeds. Keep the area watered and free of pest plants, or weeds.

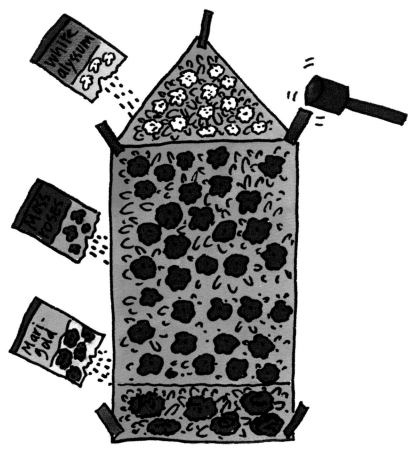

## PLANT MYSTERY

**Q.** Q. In America, a popular lawn is made from short, grassy clover. Much of the rest of the world does not have lawns at all. Yet grass makes up the largest family of plants, 25% of the earth's vegetation. **How can this be?**
(Answer on page 59.)

*continued on next page*

# PRO CHALLENGE

Until lawn games became popular and the mower was invented, American lawns were an uncut mix of grass and wildflowers. You can grow a patch the way early Americans did by simply sowing wildflower seeds in a corner of your yard that has been dug and raked smooth. Keep it watered (you won't have to weed it at all!) and see what insects you find in or near the patch. You might find:

**Ants:** There are 10 million billion (10,000,000,000,000,000) of them in the world: That's more ants than all the rest of the insect world put together!

**Bees:** A bee is said to make 3 trips for every drop of nectar it brings to the hive. Some 25,000 trips are needed to gather the raw material for 1 pound of honey.

**Butterflies:** Some kinds, such as Monarchs, can fly 35 miles (56 kilometers) an hour!

**Fireflies:** These are really a kind of male beetle. They generate light to attract a mate. A mix of oxygen and body fluids in the firefly's tail makes the glow, which is bright but not hot. The beetle controls the flow of oxygen to its tail, which in turn controls the blinking.

What other critters can you find in your wildflower patch?

# Mighty Vine Hideout

No privacy? No place to pitch a tent? No chance to go camping? No problem! Grow a living, open-sided hideout outdoors during the summer months.

## WHAT YOU NEED:

- Outdoor wall space about 3 to 4 feet (1 meter) long
- A ball of twine
- 3 bamboo support poles, each about 6 feet (2 meters) long
- Annual or perennial vining flower or vegetable seeds (see below for vine types)
- 3 clean, empty coffee cans, with drainage holes, filled with soil

*Tendril (needs a horizontal, narrow support such as a woven web of clothesline or chain-link fence): sweet pea vine, clematis, cup-and-saucer vine, green peas*

*Twining (needs a vertical support such as posts, wires, or trellis): morning glory, black-eyed Susan vine, honeysuckle, pole beans (they can grow up to 20 feet)*

*Clinging (needs a rough surface such as a brick, stone, or cement wall): ivies, trumpet creeper, Virginia creeper*

## DIRECTIONS:

1. Dig three holes about 6 inches (15 centimeters) deep and place each pole on an angle to rest against the wall. Firm the soil around the poles so that they don't wobble.
2. Your hideout is ready for planting! Sow the seeds in the soil-filled cans according to the package directions and place them against the poles. Keep the soil moist as the plants grow.
3. Tie twine from pole to pole at several heights to form a ladder.
4. As the seedlings grow, make sure they are in reach of the poles. Gently guide them to allow the vines to reach the twine. Once started, they will climb readily to the top. By late summer, you'll have a great place to hide or meet with friends.

*continued on next page*

✓ Cricket Thermometer: The warmer it is, the faster crickets chirp. You can figure out the air temperature using this fact. Here's how:

Determine the base number. You get this by first getting the current temperature outside. Then count the number of cricket chirps in 15 seconds and subtract that number from the temperature. The answer is the base number. Put this on a slip of paper somewhere where you won't lose it.

After that, any time you want to know the temperature, simply listen to the number of chirps you hear in 15 seconds, and add your base number. The answer will be the current temperature!

## PLANT MYSTERY

**Q.** Vining plants seem to defy gravity by walking up trellises and fences without much help. **How can they do this?** (Answer on page 59.)

Shape ivy vines indoors around a base of support to create a living plant design called a topiary.

## DIRECTIONS:

Fill a 6-inch pot with soil. In it, plant at least 2 or 3 ivies that are each 10 to 12 inches (25 to 30 centimeters) long. Make a topiary shape out of metal wires, glued popsicle sticks, or pipe cleaners, and insert it, upright, in the soil at the back of the pot. (Simple shapes, such as stars, hearts, and circles or trellises work best.) To train it, gently wind your ivy around the shape as it grows. Each time you work with your topiary, wash your hands because all ivies are harmful if swallowed.

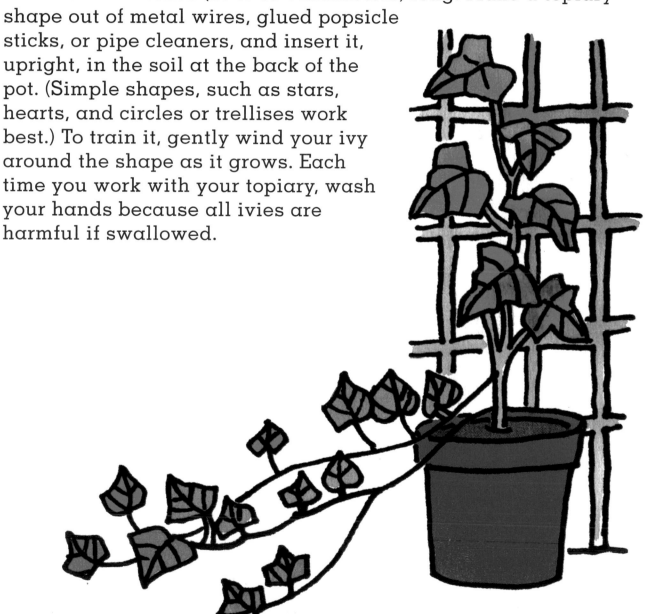

# Branching Out

Earth's oldest, biggest, and tallest living things are trees. There are about 20,000 different kinds in the world. All big trees were once little ones, called seedlings. Start a forest of your own, outdoors, one seedling at a time.

## WHAT YOU NEED:

- A closed, *dark*-colored pine cone (not green and gooey) from an evergreen
- A paper towel
- A 4-cup section from an egg carton, filled with moist, sterilized soil
- 1 gallon-sized sealable plastic bag

## DIRECTIONS:

1. Lay the pine cone on the paper towel in a warm place until it opens. (This may take several days.) Then shake the opened cone over the towel so that the seeds fall out. Choose 4 dark seeds. (Light-colored ones will not grow.)
2. Sow one seed in each cup. Press each seed lightly into the soil. Put the planted seeds in the plastic bag and place in bright, indirect light. Unless the soil becomes dry, the seeds should not be watered again until they sprout. Once the seeds have germinated (which takes about 1 month), remove the plastic bag and water until the soil is moist, not soggy.

3. When your seedlings are at least 2 inches (5 centimeters) tall, transplant each one into its own pot. Do this in the spring. For several days after planting, set the seedlings outdoors in the shade to help them get used to their new surroundings without being damaged. This process is called "hardening off." In their pots, the seedlings can grow outdoors all summer and then be planted in the ground in fall.

* While you plant, keep the seedling's roots wet and protected from wind and sun.
* Allow about 6 feet (2 meters) of space around each tree.
* Make the hole slightly larger than the width of the tree roots and about 5 inches (12 to 13 centimeters) deep.
* Once it is planted, water the young tree well and often.

*continued on next page*

## PLANT MYSTERY

**Q.** Most evergreen trees are recognizable because their leaves, called needles, grow year 'round and aren't shed all at once like the leaves of many other trees. Yet evergreen needles are often found on the ground. **What's going on?** (Answer on page 59.)

# PRO CHALLENGE

Young trees can grow rapidly. After a year or so, you may want to prune, or trim back, the tips of any unsightly branches. Pruning shapes a large plant, much as pinching back shapes smaller ones. As long as you don't cut off too much, pruning will stimulate the tree to form strong, new growth, which will give your tree a fuller look.

To cleanly cut off the tip of an unsightly branch, use a small pruning shears. Be careful not to cut yourself! Never cut the main stem, or trunk.

*Nature's tree "bomb": One kind of Mexican tree grows gourdlike seeds that are as big as oranges. When ripe, the gourds explode, shooting hard pieces up to 20 feet (6 meters) away!*

*Sources of free and/or inexpensive evergreen seedlings:*
- *The National Arbor Day Foundation*
  *100 Arbor Avenue*
  *Nebraska City, NE 68410*
  *(1-888-448-7337)*
- *your local Department of Natural Resources or U.S. Forest Service office*
- *a local, commercial paper-making company*
- *local tree or shrub nurseries*

# Wings and Stings

Grow a colorful garden for the birds, bees, and butterflies and see how many different kinds visit you!

## WHAT YOU NEED:

- Any large, old, discarded container with drainage holes, such as a washtub or windowbox (optional: a prepared garden space)
- Small rocks
- Soil
  - *Perennial plants* (from short to tall):

**For seed-eating birds:** coreopsis, black-eyed Susan, bee balm, purple coneflower, thistle

**For nectar-eating birds:** dwarf or fernleaf bleeding heart, columbine, cardinal flower, tall garden phlox

**For butterflies:** creeping phlox, sedum, butterfly weed, milkweed, aster, astilbe, butterfly bush

**For bees:** Bees are not attracted by scent—they are attracted by color. Their favorite is the color BLUE!

## DIRECTIONS:

Place your container in a sunny or partly sunny spot. Cover the bottom of the container with rocks. Then fill it with soil. With your fingers, make holes large enough for the perennials and firm the soil around them once they are in place. Make sure the taller plants are toward the back and the smaller ones are in the middle and front. Water thoroughly.

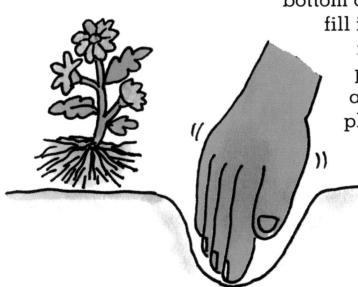

## PLANT MYSTERY

**Q.** Birds, bees, and butterflies like some plants more than others. Plants also like living next to some plants better than others. **What causes this?**
(Answer on page 60.)

*Most monarch butterflies fly to Mexico for the winter months. For some of them, that's 2,500 miles (4,000 kilometers) in 6 weeks. Milkweed juices make the monarch poisonous to birds. Monarchs that eat milkweed aren't affected, but birds that eat these monarchs get sick.*

## PRO  CHALLENGE

Perennials flower and then produce seeds, which can either be left on the plant as bird food or collected and saved to sow the following spring. Seeds are ready to collect when they become brown and dried. Do not collect them in wet weather (for best results, the outdoor humidity plus air temperature should equal a number less than 100). Put the seeds into a sealable plastic bag and store them in a refrigerator until needed for planting in early spring. Moldy seeds will not germinate and must be discarded.

# Sneaker Feet

Don't toss away that old, blown-out sneaker! Recycle it.

## WHAT YOU NEED:

- An old sneaker
- A sturdy plastic bag to fit inside the shoe
- Sterilized soil
- Pebbles
- Small green annual plants:
  **Sun-lovers:** marigolds, petunias, and snapdragon
  **Shade-lovers:** impatiens, pansies, and vinca vine

## DIRECTIONS:

1. Fit the opened plastic bag inside the shoe. Pull the tongue forward. (For an outdoor planter, poke a few holes in the bag first, to allow water to drain out.)

2. To keep plant roots from rotting, sprinkle a layer of pebbles, 1/2 inch (1 centimeter) deep, inside the plastic bag.
3. Add 1 inch (2 1/2 centimeters) of soil, then place the annuals inside the shoe opening.
4. Use more soil to fill in any spaces around the plants.
5. Carefully dampen the soil with a little water so that it is moist, not soggy. (Indoors, don't water again until the top of the soil is dry to the touch. Outdoors, check the soil every day, especially in hot weather).

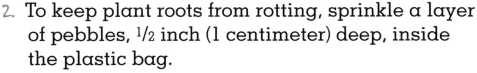

6. Depending on which plants you've chosen, put the finished sneaker planter in either sun or shade.

## PLANT MYSTERY

**Q.** After a few days, the plants in your sneaker will begin to lean and grow toward the light. **Why does this happen?** (Answer on page 60.)

# PRO CHALLENGE

Your feet aren't the only things that may outgrow your sneaker. When the flowers grow wild and your shoe seems to disappear, it's time to repot the plants.

Fill a 6- to 8-inch flowerpot halfway with soil. Carefully lift the plastic liner from the sneaker, and pull it away from the soil and roots. Discard the plastic. Place the root ball with plants into the pot. Follow directions 4 through 6 for the Sneaker Feet project above.

# Making Scents

Herbs are plants that were used from earliest times in food, as medicines, and in personal grooming. Here, they'll wake up your taste buds and wow your sense of smell!

## WHAT YOU NEED:

- A large unused toy such as a sandpail or the bed of a dumptruck
- Sterilized soil
- 6 popsicle sticks, each labeled with the name of an herb
- A pinch of each of these seeds: thyme, chives, parsley,** sage, basil, and oregano

> **Parsley seeds take several weeks to germinate. Be patient!

- *Thyme, an evergreen, is a natural antiseptic used in mouthwash and toothpaste.*
- *Chives, which taste like onions, have been around almost 3,000 years.*
- *Ancient Greeks fed parsley to their horses before battle to make them brave.*
- *Sage was once thought to improve memory and give wisdom to those who ate it.*
- *When stepped on, crushed basil sweetened the air in sickrooms in medieval times.*
- *Long ago, oregano was a Greek toothache medicine.*

## DIRECTIONS:

1. Fill the sandpail with soil, leaving about ½ inch (1 centimeter) of space at the top. Moisten the surface. With a finger, indent the soil into six pie-shaped areas. Following the directions on the seed packages, sow the seeds, one type to each area. Mark each area with its labeled stick.

2. Gently water the soil so that it is moist but not soggy. Allow it to dry slightly between waterings while the seeds sprout.

3. Place the herb pot in a sunny window indoors or outdoors in late spring after the last frost. Since the pail has no drainage, protect it from heavy rain. Once the seeds sprout, be sure to turn the pail every few days to compensate for phototropism.

4. When the young herbs are about 6 inches (15 centimeters) high, you'll notice a delicious scent as you pass by. Rub your fingers across the leaves. This helps to release essential oils.

5. Begin snipping off bits of growth to add to cooking. (You can safely pinch off up to half the growth without harming the plant.) In a few months, your pot will be full to the brim with fresh, great-smelling herbs.

✓ Feed Me! Improve the flavor and quality of your herb plants. Combine 2 tablespoons of mixed dried herbs (or 1 cup of fresh mixed herbs) with 4 cups (1 liter) of very hot water. Allow to steep for 10 minutes, then strain and cool. Once a month, water your herbs with this health tea.

## PLANT MYSTERY

**Q.** Instead of being harmed, herbs that have been pinched back (by half of their growth or less) grow thick and healthy. **Why?** (Answer on page 60.)

## PRO CHALLENGE

Sow catnip or oat grass seeds in a clean, unused pet dish that is filled with moist sterilized soil. Cover with plastic wrap and place in a sunny window. When the seeds germinate, remove the plastic wrap and water whenever the soil is dry to the touch. Leave it where kitty can munch without making a mess. Because catnip can grow five feet (1½ meters) tall or more, pinch it back.

# Fruit o' the Room

Grow your own strawberry crop and enjoy the fruit of your labor.

## WHAT YOU NEED:

- 1 medium-sized lampshade
- 4 strawberry plants, found at garden centers
- Heavy plastic for a liner
- Moist sterilized soil
- Scissors
- Drainage saucer

## DIRECTIONS:

1. Turn the lampshade upside-down. Line the inside with plastic and poke holes for drainage in the bottom.
2. Fill the lampshade with soil and scoop one hole for each plant. Place each plant, one to a hole, so that the roots hang straight down and the crown, or center growth, is just above the surface of the soil. (See the figure for correct planting depth).
3. Firm the soil around the roots, being careful not to bury the crown.
4. Place the drainage saucer beneath the lampshade and place in direct sunlight. Keep the plants well-watered.
5. After the last frost, the lampshade planter can be put outdoors in a sunny place. Remember to keep the soil moist.

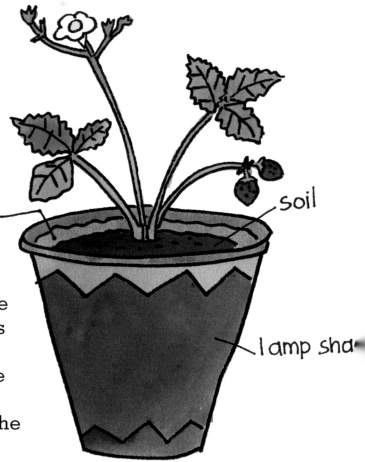

plastic

soil

lamp sha

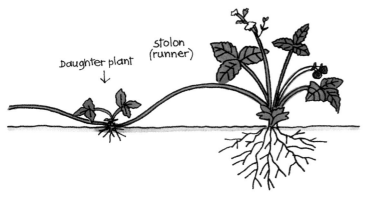

Daughter plant

stolon (runner)

6. Strawberry plants send out runners, called stolons, which grow new plants. These new babies are called daughter plants. Once the daughter plant's root is formed, you can snip the plant free from the stolon and put it in its own container.

✓ Getting the Berry Best Results: Fertilize strawberry plants every 2 weeks with a plant food that dissolves in water. (These are found at discount and garden centers.)

✓ Seedy Characters: Unlike many other fruits, strawberry seeds grow on the outside. They are the light-colored specks found in the many pits on the strawberry's skin.

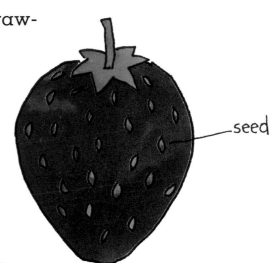

seed

## PLANT MYSTERY

**Q.** Like other outdoor perennials, strawberries like a layer of mulch around them. **How does mulching help these plants?** (Answer on page 60.)

## PRO CHALLENGE

You can keep your strawberry's daughter plants for next year by growing them outdoors in a prepared, sunny garden space. A layer of natural mulch, or ground covering, such as weed-free straw or shredded bark, will help to keep these plants healthy all year long. Spread the mulch around the plants, not over them, and no deeper than a finger's depth. Keep the plants well watered, especially in hot weather.

# All Wet!

Use these wet-footed plants to make a miniature marsh.

## WHAT YOU NEED:

- A medium-sized plastic dishpan with drainage holes (This is the planter.)
- A larger plastic dishpan without drainage holes (this is the saucer)
- Equal amounts of peat moss and soil, mixed together
- Small rocks or pebbles
- Water
- 3 or 4 moisture-loving perennial plants chosen from (short to tall): vinca, ajuga, anemone, hosta, turtle-heads, astilbe, and trollius

## DIRECTIONS:

1. Fill the soil mixture in the medium dishpan about an inch below the edge. With your hand, scoop out 3 or 4 hollows in the soil.

Peat Moss + Soil

Pebbles + water

2. Place a plant in each hole and firm the soil around the roots.

3. Pour a 2-inch (5-centimeter) layer of pebbles in the bottom of the large dishpan and fill it halfway with water. Slowly set the planter into the water. The soil will then absorb water through the plants' roots. Place your mini-marsh in a partly shady area.

4. Refill the saucer with water only when the pebbles are exposed. Whenever it rains, take the planter out of the saucer to prevent the plants from flooding.

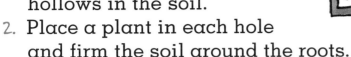

## PLANT MYSTERY

**Q. Why will any plant, even a moisture-loving one, die if it gets waterlogged?**
(Answer on page 60.)

## PRO CHALLENGE

When any of the moisture-loving perennials in this project outgrows its container, you can easily divide the clump to create new plants. To do this, carefully dig the plant up and gently remove the soil to see root clumps. You'll notice areas of new growth. The plant can be pulled or cut apart at these places. (If you use a knife, be sure to ask an adult to help you.) As soon as possible, plant all the clumps in their own pots or prepared space in a partly shady garden.

# Something's Rotten!

Feed your indoor houseplants your own compost tea. It will be ready to use in 4 to 6 weeks.

## WHAT YOU NEED:

- 2 empty 3-pound margarine tubs with lids
- A new wooden pencil, sharpened
- A ballpoint pen
- 3 cups of vegetable peelings, shredded. (Fruit peelings should not be used *indoors*, or you'll have a fruitfly motel.)
- ½ cup of unsterilized garden soil
- 2 cups water
- A ruler
- A spoon
- A clean, empty gallon milk jug with a cap

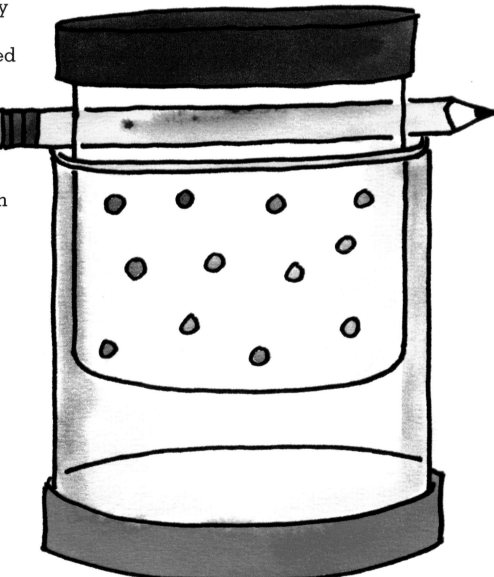

# DIRECTIONS:

1. Working in or near the kitchen sink, place a lid on one of the tubs (this is the composter). Poke as many large holes in the lid as you can (without splitting it) with the ballpoint pen. Then turn the tub upside-down and poke lots of holes into the bottom.

2. Still using the composter, measure 1 inch (2½ centimeters) below the container's rim. From one side, poke the pencil through the middle until it comes out the other side. Leave the pencil in place. At pencil level and above, poke additional air holes with your pen all the way around the composter without splitting the sides or getting too close to the pencil holes.

3. Remove the lid from the other tub. (This is the drainage tub.) Nest the composter within the drainage tub so that the pencil rests on the upper edge. Place the lid without holes underneath the drainage tub.

4. Take off the lid with holes from the composter. Fill the composter with veggie peelings, soil, and water and stir until the peelings are coated and the water drips into the drainage tub. (This will be the liquid tea.) Put the lid with holes onto the composter and put it in a sunny, warm place. Stir daily.

*continued on next page*

5. Once a week, take the composter out of the drainage tub. Set it on top of the drainage lid and pour the collected liquid tea back into the compost. Quickly place the composter back into the drainage tub before the tea drains through. Stir thoroughly with the spoon. Do this for a month or until the veggie scraps look and smell earthy.

6. Fill the milk jug halfway with water and add the compost tea. Put the cap on, and shake. Use it to water the soil of your houseplants.
The organic matter left in your composter can be added to soil when potting.

Compost tea

## PLANT MYSTERY

**Q. Why is unsterilized soil good for composting?** (answer on page 60.)

## PRO CHALLENGE

An outdoor compost pile started in the fall, when you have access to both leaves and grass (after you've jumped on them, of course), will be ready to use by spring.

54

# WHAT YOU NEED:

- Green plant material (old plants, grass clippings, green leaves, and weeds)
- Brown plant material (fall leaves, old straw, and other dried plant material)
- Fruit and vegetable peelings (See list of *do's* to compost)
- Unsterilized garden soil
- A shovel
- A pitchfork
- An unused sunny or shady area of your yard for the compost pile (about the size of a sandbox, located near a handy water source).

# DIRECTIONS:

1. Collect equal amounts of small, chopped green and brown plant materials. Spread them and kitchen scraps or peelings in thin layers until there is a 10- to 12-inch-high (25 to 30 centimeters) pile.
2. Add 2 or 3 shovelsful of soil. Water the pile so that it's moist like a sponge.
3. Once a week, turn your pile over with a pitchfork. Add green and brown materials and kitchen scraps as often as you like. Make sure to always add your materials in thin layers and add 2 or 3 shovelsful of soil for every 10 to 12 inches (25 to 30 centimeters).
4. Add water so that the compost is moist.
5. Your compost is ready when it looks, smells, and feels like dark, crumbly soil. Sift out any chunks that have not decomposed fully before using the compost on growing plants. Usually, 1 to 3 months is needed to get good compost. Keeping the pile moist and turning it often will speed up the composting process.

*continued on next page*

- Layering a compost pile allows microorganisms to decompose, or break down, the materials into humus more quickly.

- The pile will start to heat up, or cook, and decompose within 1 week.

- Cover your pile with an old carpet or plastic tarp during long periods of rain or snow so that it doesn't get waterlogged. (A compost pile never learns to swim.)

- Turning everything upside-down keeps the contents from sticking together and smelling bad. A bad smell means that your pile is too wet and isn't getting enough oxygen. Add more dry contents to your pile and mix together thoroughly to fix this problem.

- Keep your compost pile out of direct view of your and your neighbors' windows and away from wooden structures where heat and moisture might rot the wood. But keep it where it will be protected from being blown away.

- Some states, cities, and towns have regulations on composting. Check with your Department of Natural Resources and local zoning office to find out if there are any regulations in your area. Most of these rules are set to keep an area disease-free and safe from animal pests.

## DO'S OF COMPOSTING OUTDOORS:
- Grass clippings (not treated with herbicides or pesticides)
- Old plants (from the house or garden, disease-free)
- Flowers
- Chopped fruit and vegetable peels, stalks, and leaves
- Shredded green and dried leaves
- Pine needles (Use small amounts—they decompose slowly.)
- Crushed eggshells
- Coffee grounds
- Shredded newspaper (black-and-white only)

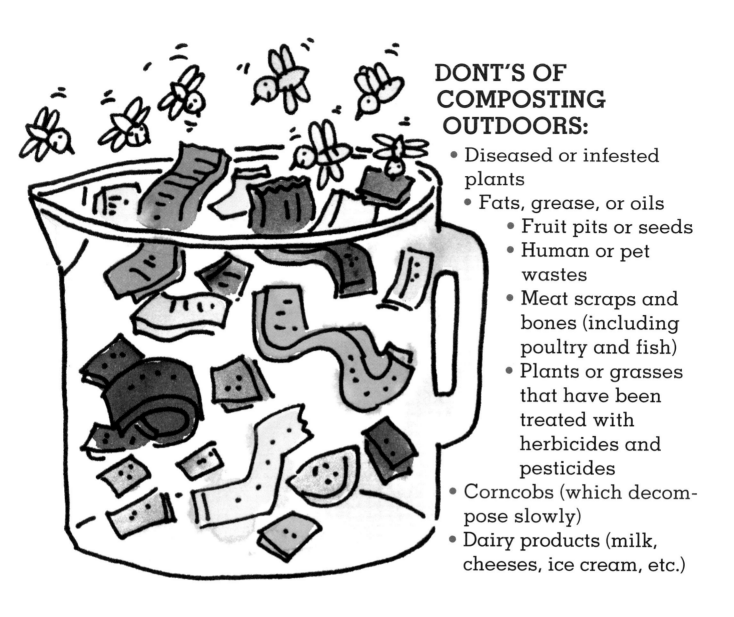

## DONT'S OF COMPOSTING OUTDOORS:

- Diseased or infested plants
  - Fats, grease, or oils
    - Fruit pits or seeds
    - Human or pet wastes
    - Meat scraps and bones (including poultry and fish)
    - Plants or grasses that have been treated with herbicides and pesticides
- Corncobs (which decompose slowly)
- Dairy products (milk, cheeses, ice cream, etc.)

## TOP REASONS TO COMPOST:

- Hungry microorganisms will always know where to go for their midnight snack.
- Your family will assume that there really is alien life (and you've been "taken over" by it) when you rake the lawn without being asked.
- When someone asks whether you can "cook," you won't be lying!
- You can give your garbage disposal the day off.
- Waste not today, and your plants will want not tomorrow.

# Answers to Plant Mysteries

## SPROUT OFF

Even though it may look dry and dead, every living seed is a self-contained plant, ready to grow. The hard outer shell protects the inner baby plant, but it can still breathe and take in water. With water, warmth, and sometimes light, the hard outer seed coat softens and the plant emerges.

## CUTTING LOOSE

A cutting's leaves provide food, which leads to new growth and the formation of mature plant parts, such as roots. This is done by photosynthesis, a process that turns sunlight, water, plant nutrients, and carbon dioxide into food energy. Even well-rooted plants rely on photosynthesis, because a plant's leaves are the only known way to turn sun energy into food energy.

## LOOK' IN GLASS

A correctly balanced terrarium imitates the pattern of a rain cycle. The plants take in moisture from the soil through their roots and respire in the form of vapor through their leaves. This vapor collects on the inside of the glass. This moisture, called condensation, trickles down and is reabsorbed by the soil, keeping it damp but not too wet. There should be only enough moisture in the container to nurture the plants and continue this natural cycle. If there is more, the plant roots will rot.

## IT'S A DRY LIFE

Succulents protect themselves against animal and weather dangers in several ways:
1. Cactus leaves are sharp spines, and the stems are green, fleshy, and thick-skinned. Succulents have tough, strong, thick-skinned leaves that lose little moisture to the dry air and are difficult for animals to eat.
2. They grow in rocks or trees out of reach.
3. They camouflage themselves, or blend into their surroundings, which can make animals overlook them.
4. To keep from overheating or drying up, some plants bury themselves almost completely, then let light in through exposed "windows" in their leaf tips.
5. Some make poisonous juices that animals won't swallow.

## WINTER LIGHT BULBS

After the plant has bloomed, food for next spring is produced in the leaves and transferred to the bulb for storage. After the food storage period, the bulb slows down its growth and the leaves are no longer needed. They turn yellow and dry up. Removing a bulb's leaves too soon stops the plant's ability to store food needed for next year's flowers.

## LETTUCE EAT

To germinate, healthy garden seeds need these things: warmth, water, oxygen, and sometimes light. While stored on the shelf, the seed can still "breathe," but unless it receives water, it won't begin to grow. Sometimes, seeds get wet accidentally or a lot of moisture from the air seeps into the seed. This causes germination before the proper time. That's why directions on seed packets tell you to store the seeds in a cool, dry place until they are needed.